T0147323

Thoughts That Come From Growing Old

THADDEUS J. WILLIAMS

iUniverse, Inc.
Bloomington

Thoughts That Come From Growing Old

iUniverse books may be ordered through booksellers or by contacting:

iUniverse
1663 Liberty Drive
Bloomington, IN 47403
www.iuniverse.com
1-800-Authors (1-800-288-4677)

ISBN: 978-1-4502-8438-7 (pbk)
ISBN: 978-1-4502-8439-4 (cloth)
ISBN: 978-1-4502-8440-0 (ebk)

Printed in the United States of America

iUniverse rev. date: 2/10/11

DEDICATION

I would like to dedicate this book to my parents, the late Lawrence S. Williams, and Sarah E. Williams for all of their hard work for putting four children through college in the sixties. We know the task was not easy, but we all endured.

To them I say thanks for a job well done.

I would also like to thank the late Dr. O. P. Lowe, Vice President Emeritus, Mississippi Valley State University, and his wife Mrs. Henri E. Lowe who in part were responsible for my education.

This book is written about some of the many sayings I have heard across the years. Many of the people were elderly, and I thought the the sayings were strange, so I began writing them down when I was about fifteen years old. Some of the sayings got lost across the years, but I managed to keep up with most of them.

These sayings cover the United States, Canada, Mexico, and Hawaii. Some of the thoughts are my own, and some are not. I hope you will enjoy reading them.

Thoughts That Come From Growing Old

by

THADDEUS J. WILLIAMS

I am defined by my experiences and accomplishments while on this journey through life. How do you define yourself? What will your legacy be?

Faith will never let you down if you believe.

A perfect love will cover a multitude of faults.

There is never healing in hatred and anger, nor is there any love.

Never let anyone tell you that you won't amount to nothing. Always prove them wrong, and tell them about you're success story.

Always remember, God is always on call for what ever you need he's only a thought away. He who abides in God, God will abide in him. Never put God last in your life. You have been blessed in ways you have never thought of. Make it a date to talk to God daily and watch the blessings unfold in your life. All you have to do is believe, is that so hard to do?

When you find out who you really are, then you will learn how to love someone else. Real life is not a cat and mouse game.

The truth always poses a threat to power.

Always stand up for what's right, then you're really standing tall.

Have you ever stopped to consider that many people get treated the way they allow themselves to be treated? Only you can stop the vicious circle.

It's always good to have a college education, but it's even greater to be rich in common sense.

He who knows he knows is a wise man, he who think he knows is fool. Why not get it right the first time.

A guilty conscious needs no accuser.

There are two kinds of people, explosive, and implosive. Explosive people are those that let things go, they just blow up. Implosive people are those that keep things to themselves, and sometimes suffer because they are afraid to let loose.

Never loose your dependency on youth, it's what keeps you motivated and going.

If you don't believe in anything, it is the very reason that you will fail at what you attempt to do in life.

You don't need a wishbone, you have a backbone, use it God is in you.

If you want to be healed and be blessed, ask God to for what ever it is that you need. Long drawn out prayers are not required. God knows what you need before you ask. The simpler the prayer, the better.

Don't worry about what people call you, it's what you answer to that will get you ahead in life.

Nothing comes to a sleeper but a dream. Dream the impossible and make it a reality. Makers and shakers rule the world.

To him who is given much, much is required.

If you want a true friend and a confidant, God is only a breath away.

The way you present yourself in most cases will tell a great deal about your character.

Did you know the greatest sin is fear?

A willful waste makes an awful want. Therefore waste not, want not.

Be a decision maker for yourself, make quality sound decisions. Stay around positive people, it makes a difference.

Partner with God, and keep committed.

Don't hate the player, hate the game. Every game has a winner.

What ever you think and believe, you will achieve.

The easiest thing in the world to do is finding fault in others.

I'm looking for someone to walk with me that someone is Jesus can you help me find him?

Marriage can be defined in three ways. Selective, Objective, and Convenience. Which is yours? Do you know the difference?

Little leaks can sink big ships don't let your faith be lost by little leaks. Keep the faith and remain strong.

Science can only go so far, then comes God.

How do you loose yourself to someone, but you don't loose your way?

Never question the motive, question the judgment behind the motive.

The eyes are the window to the soul, be aware of what you perceive.

An active mind is a mind in progress, positive or negative.

There is never a cause for action for good or bad advice. You can either accept or reject it. The choice is yours.

The most dangerous person in the world is the liar.

If you perceive something as not being right and you cannot come to a final conclusion delete it from your life and move on.

Always believe in yourself, and be competitive.

Always keep the integrity of who you are, and the things that make you happy, then your life will be complete.

The sore has to hurt before it can heal, patience is a virtue.

A fair swop is no swindle.

Real love is the labor of life between husband and wife when you have been together for numerous years, you know the fabric that kept you together.

Learn to put limits on friendships especially when it pertains to money. It's okay. to say no. This will stop the frustration, and the worrying about will I ever get my money back? This can apply to other situations as well.

When we know better, we should do better.

Every thing in life is on its way somewhere. We are on a journey just passing through. Where will your journey lead you?

A vision without a plan is an has lunation.

A part of every person's illness is worrying about it, that won't help the problem. Pray to God to heal your illness then move on. Remember God never lost a case.

You will never discover new horizons if you are afraid to leave the shore.

Life is short, be all that you can be and leave a positive legacy for others to follow.

If you cannot achieve what you attempt, be brave in what you do.

Be careful of who you love, you could be hurt or killed.

Meaningful actions require meaningful thoughts.

Wisdom is fully understood when you have gone through the personal trials and tribulations and the defeat in your life. Then comes the understanding of what you are to do that will make an impact on your life and in someone else's.

He who lives dangerously will in most cases die dangerously.

Always listen to your own mind, and no one can steer you in the wrong direction.

How much trust can you put in a friend when you know they have arterial motives? Most so called friends want to be a friend because they think they can use you to gain what they really want or need. How many friends you know like that?

You were born with the innate ability to know right from wrong. Always listen to what your inner spirit tells you.

Love is stronger than any addiction in the world, it never fails.

You can always inform a person, but you cannot transform them. They have to do this on their own.

In some cases words won't help you, only actions will heal the wound.

Always pray in the spirit, and ask for divine enlightenment.

Cheaters never prosper, and liars are never to be trusted.

The truth is as old as God, and will endure as long as he. The right will prevail, the wrong will fail.

Learn not to doubt, it can change an outcome. It's ok to be aggressive, but only in a positive way.

If you listen for God to inspire you, you will be lead in the right direction, and it won't be easy. Temptation comes in all forms.

While on this journey through life, learn to live the good life. The body wick burns shorter each day. Man is mortal, and man did not create you, nor can he save you. God will be the final judge, not man.

No one ever have your best interest at heart, someone you know is always after something usually monetary. Learn to be a good listener, and watch everything.

Family members can be the worst members of any group. How much love is in your family?

When your friends gossip to you about others, you can rest assured they will gossip about you to.

When you don't have anything, you don't need anything.

Many people are influenced by what they are told, some by what they see.

It's strange we never appreciate what we had until we finally miss it.

Remember, if you are not true to your teeth they will be false to you.

I will never understand why we fight for freedom in other countries when we barely have our own. Many citizens of this country are not free as they should be as defined by the United States Constitution. The battle for freedom need to be fought here in the United States, especially for injustice, and other related reforms.

Always keep a personal circle of trust. It may not consist of more than two people, but let it be people you can trust with your life.

Love is stronger than revenge. It will never let you down.

Some things can be sensed, not explained. I wonder why?

Ignorance and despair is why some people do what the do.

Keep your problems to yourself, don't include me in them I have enough of my own.

Learn to feed on knowledge.

Always plan your work, then work your plan.

Strange, we never think about the victim until we become one.

Live to stay free of distractions, they cloud your mind.

Everyone have the right to his or her own opinion, but we all need to be considerate of others. You might miss out on a valuable lesson on life.

Corruption for some people is always the order for the day. Anyone can be a victim especially the elderly.

To be free in mind, body, and spirit is the only way you can say you are indeed a free person.

Never be jealous of anyone what will being jealous of another person's success do for you other than making you sick. Learn to do things for yourself, it will make you a better person.

I have found through observation that a vast majority of people make a big mistake simply because they use the terminology they said or they told me. If you want to know the truth about something, investigate the facts for yourself then come to your own conclusion.

Don't get caught up in hear- say or any un-truth. You will always find yourself defending against something you did not say.

Never be so fast as to jump to defend another person. That jump could lead you to a life of misery.

It's okay to be used, but not misused. Learn the difference between the two. People take too much for granted these days.

Learn how to make an attitude call into gratitude. Jot down the things that make you angry with yourself and with others. Keep a journal of the things that make you happy and at ease with yourself, and the things that frustrate you. These two list can and will make you a more thoughtful person.

Never use the word can't in your vocabulary, we are crippled enough as it is.

Every time someone throws you a curve ball in life, make it a grand slam. You're sending a message. You won't be put down, used, or defeated.

Learn something new ever day it helps keep the mind active and stimulated.

Under religious doctrine, if you believe in God, you have a right to the tree of life. By no means, can anyone give it to you. You have to earn this right like everyone else. I suggest that you get busy now, for time is at hand.

Never be satisfied with anything, investigate the circumstances and the conditions. It could make or break you, always think before you speak.

In the midst of any situation, learn to go back to the source of the problem, then you will find the solution to the problem.

Life is simple when we take time to understand it. Try to figure out the greatest mystery of life, then learn to be at piece with yourself.

Always be careful of what you say about people, or what you do to people. Bad Karma will make you wish you were dead.

I have often wondered how many people realize that they have written themselves a one way first class ticket to Hell, no refund. What you say, and what you do, and how you treat people is a real problem. How can you justify this?

One good thing about being wrong is the joy it brings to others. The next time you are wrong, watch the facial expressions of others as they gloat.

In this walk of life, I have found it amusing and pitiful that some people will let others take full control of their life. They will tell you what to do, when to do it, and how it is to be done. I say to those people take full control of your own life. Be an independent thinker. We all make mistakes in life. In short, be the master of your fate, and the captain of your own soul. Follow your own destiny.

Never be so caught up in other peoples business and affairs leaving your own business un-attended and un-done.

Never be jealous of someone's good fortune in life, I'm sure they had to work for it just like everyone else did. Nothing in life is free. If you want the good life, do like every one else work for it.

Be not afraid of the unknown, it is simply what it is the unknown.

We have all feared death at some point in our lives, I have come to the conclusion that it is merely crossing from one horizon to another.

Never wright off any one, they could be a God send, and you could miss the blessing of a lifetime. You will never know who God will send to you to bring you a blessing. The obvious is not always noticed.

Learn to save change. Pennies make nickels, nickels make dimes, and dimes make dollars. It all adds up.

Have you ever heard the term this is your egg? You hatch it.

Never tear down another person's dream if possible, help to build them up, or at least send them in the right direction for completion.

In this life, learn to make every disappointment, every set back, and every failure a challenge. Failure is success turned in side out a heavy dark cloud with a tint of doubt so stick to the fight when you're hardest hit it's when trouble arise you never quit.

Determine for yourself if the cup is half full or half empty. Be a decision maker.

People need to learn to use their head for more than a hat rack or an empty lot. Develop the space between your ears.

Which body part is the most important? .Why do you think so?

Nothing is so complicated that it cannot be understood.

The greatest need for all people is common sense. It will get you moving in the right direction.

Never let anyone infringe upon your constitutional rights. Everyone is equal under the law. Never be tricked or forced into doing anything you know is wrong.

Everyone is wise until he speaks.

Never try to fill other peoples shoes you have enough trouble trying to keep your shoes on your own feet.

If you keep going around in circles, you will never make it to the road of recovery.

We will always have adversity in life, if you are a resilient person nothing can hold you down.

Every one needs somebody or someone at some point and time in life. No one can go through life alone.

Always pay attention to your world around you. You will be surprised at what you will learn, pay close attention to detail.

Never think to highly of yourself, or where you come from. When you fall from grace, and have to come home, your friends and neighbors won't know you, or they won't have anything to do with you. Don't burn the bridge you may have to cross one day.

Don't dwell on the past, you cannot change what has happened. Learn from your mistakes and move on. Life is for living.

Always take the responsibility for the choices you make in life, don't look for excuses or blame others.

Never bind yourself into something you cannot get out of. The world is full of treacherous people.

What is your position in life? Are you a leader or a follower? Which ever it is, be the best at what you do.

I have discovered after many years of helping people the best revenge in life is living well, especially when people are jealous of you and most times for no reason at all. I know this to be true because it has happened to me on numerous occasions. The journey through life is the greater teacher.

If God is truly in a man's heart all things are possible.

How many people have you helped while on your journey through life? How many have stopped to say thanks for the help?

Wisdom and knowledge are the principle things, therefore get wisdom and knowledge, and with all thy getting, get understanding. If you don't have understanding you don't have anything. All three work hand and hand.

Never stop dreaming, no one knows what the final frontier holds.

Tough times don't last long. You never had to wander in the wilderness forty years.

The most precious time of all is the time you spend with your family. Please use that time wisely, it cannot be retrieved, but it can be remembered.

Never live by other peoples' standards. This is why they fall into the failure trap. Plot your own course and make adjustments as needed.

Always be the person you want to be, and not the person someone else want you to be.

Crime is contagious. That's why the prisons stay full. Think about it.

Always remember, there is life until death so please live your life. Death is the final destination in this world as we know it.

Never worry about anything you don't have control of it's useless, and all you are going to do is make yourself sick worrying about it.

The choices you make in life will define who you really are, so choose well.

Always be the leading person in your own life story, after all you are the one telling it.

If you don't know something to be true, why in the world do you think gossip is going to make it right?

The truth crushed away in the face of the earth will always rise again even in the Blind scale of justice. True faith and justice will prevail as it pertains to justice. How many men and women have been convicted unjustly? The numbers are staggering.

I have never understood why some people think that they are so much better than others. I guess I can attribute this to how people were raised as children, and it is a carry over from one generation to the next. If we don't learn to treat all people as human beings with dignity and respect, this old world as we know it will soon implode. Many people have been dealt an un-just hand for no reason at all.

Have you ever stopped to consider taking a complete inventory of your life? What makes you happy, or will it do just the opposite. Think about how much good you have done for others, or if you have not done enough. Why not make your life better than it really is. You can make a difference, after all it's your life.

When talking to so called friends, pay close attention as to what they have to say. Many times, things are not what you perceive them to be.

Why do some people lie just for the sake of lying? These people bare watching at all times, and they never can be trusted for any reason. How many people do you know like this? They always want to be the center of attention. Apparently they don't know how foolish they sound or look.

I have learned the hard way that we are not obligated to any one. We generally do things to help someone because we want to, not because we have to.

Always remember, when you put your trust in someone it should never to be taken lightly. To trust someone is a serious matter. One day your life might depend on it.

Never say what you will or you won't eat. Hunger will make a Monkey eat red pepper. Mother knows best.

To all men and women who are having a tough time with your mate, and they seem not to be pulling their fair share of the load I say to you, drop that zero and find yourself a hero. Everyone can do much better if they only try.

Have you ever stopped to consider that many people get treated the way they allow themselves to be treated? Is it low self esteem? Or are you afraid to speak up for yourself?

If you cannot be truthful to anybody, be truthful to yourself. It's a beginning in the right direction.

Never try to make your friends look stupid while you try to steal the lime light. The last laugh will be on you. Play fair, and avoid embarrassment, it happens all the time. Learn to control your temper an apology won't heal broken bones. Once the damage is done, it's done. Sometimes it's best to just walk away. It won't make you any less of a human being.

In all things give thinks, you could be gone in the blink of an eye.

Never forget the greatest mistake in life is giving up. If you give up what have you accomplished? Absolutely nothing.

Always remember, turning your back on God is your own peril.

Have you ever noticed that some people like to belittle others, and while in the process they make themselves look stupid. They seem to have the answer to every thing.

Never compromise on a lifetime commitment if it is something you really want to do. In the end, who do you blame?

I will never understand why some people always want to be the tough guy, when deep down you can see that they are some of the the loneliest people in the world. You can actually see that they want compassion, and companionship, or just to belong, and are afraid to ask for help. Stubbornness is a sickness also.

There is no such thing as a disparate situation. You knew what you were doing when you got into trouble, common sense will tell you, you should not have done it in the first place.

Children are the greatest imitators of their parents. What are you teaching your children?

Education begins at home, not in the classroom. Always delete the negative, and be a good role model, and help your children in all aspects of their lives. A positive attitude will bring a positive and good developmental foundation in your child's life. Delete the negative, and accentuate the positive. Children imitate what they see and hear.

You cannot blame anyone other than yourself for your actions. Always remember, what you do in life or with your life is your responsibility. The blame game will never work, it's a cheap cop-out.

Always remember, it takes two to get married, and it takes two to keep it to together. Dedication and commitment is the key to a life time of marriage.

Do the good out weigh the bad in your life? Think about it. I'm sure you know the answer.

Always be aware of mind manipulators, or the people who play the confidence game.

If something sounds too good to be true and you fall for the line, you have just been had. It only takes a few seconds to hold your attention. With these type people simply say I'm not interested and keep moving.

Never wait on someone to do everything for you all the time. You will be bound for the rest of your life. Break the chains of laziness and do things for yourself.

Did you know that most people use only ten percent of their brain? and some even less. What a waist.

I have often wondered how many thousands of people work at thankless jobs. Your boss never tells you how much you are appreciated, or keep up the good work. Think about it.

Always remember, you can lie to mankind, but not to God.

Man can forgive man. Only God can make it divine forgiveness.

Will we ever understand it is easier to tell the truth as opposed to telling a lie?

I was told by an elderly deceased friend that there is such a thing as joy in sorrow. After all, you do have the memories

Have you ever stopped to consider what is deep down inside of you at your core? That inner spirit that drives you. I urge you to stop and listen to what it tells you. You could be pleasantly surprised.

Try to stay away from the name calling game. You would not want anyone to talk about you and your family. Learn to put skid chains on your tongue. Name calling cuts like a double edge sword.

Always remember, dreams do come true if you believe.

In your deepest hour of dispair, and you feel that God has given up on you, remain strong in your faith. God is the master planner, miracles happen every day. Never forget that God is an one time God, and you cannot rush perfection. God will see you through your problem what ever it is.

I hope that this little book can be of some help to someone along the way. It has been an inspiration for me to put it together. I hope you the reader will enjoy the sayings, and refer to them from time to time. It might just be the medicine you need.